"To read this collection of poems from Sam Sax is to be inside the animal, the lyric *i* inside the word *pig*. Through otherwise occidental history and personal experience, Sax seductively tracks and uses porcine manifestations as correlatives for rendering desire, the desire to be known, and the systems of power that threaten such knowledge. These poems are animated, and reanimated, by a queer and queenly sonic intelligence that wrestles with itself and, ultimately, reaches for the hope required to persist. 'all i. want is. to live,' the speaker says. '& live.'"

—Paul Tran, author of *All the Flowers Kneeling*

"In *Pig*, Sam Sax charts a complicated and haunting portrayal of body, home, desire, nation, and beast. Sax is able to weave humor throughout their invention, creating new lyrical and visual terrain for language, for connection, for feeling, and for possibility. This book invites you in and then winds through the labyrinths of the mind, body, and history. Sax's words open and open, creating a space of examination of the pig in so many forms. As soon as I started reading the book I could not stop; these are poems that I could build a home in."

—Fatimah Asghar, author of *When We Were Sisters*

"There are few things I love more in writing than the absolute pleasure(s) of multiple considerations—a writer who holds an object in their hand and turns it over, tenderly, affording an audience a look at their obsession from several angles. Sam Sax takes this to heights that only they are capable of in *Pig*, dissecting shape, sound, multiple etymologies, histories. These are poems as rich in playfulness as they are in heartbreak. But they shine in their relentless curiosity. 'grief is an animal' is beautiful all on its own, but it is the questioning that follows—what kind of animal? let's cut to the chase, after all."

—Hanif Abdurraqib, author of *A Little Devil in America*

"In this deeply lyrical and experimental tour de force, Sax smashes and inspects every interchangeable lens of the pig, literal and figurative, to unflinchingly examine sexuality, grief, xenotransplantation, and the nature of language itself. Biblical and humorous, provocative and tragic, these poems evoke an absolute and necessary understanding of the very boundaries of our humanity."

—Richard Blanco, author of *How to Love a Country*

SCRIBNER POETRY

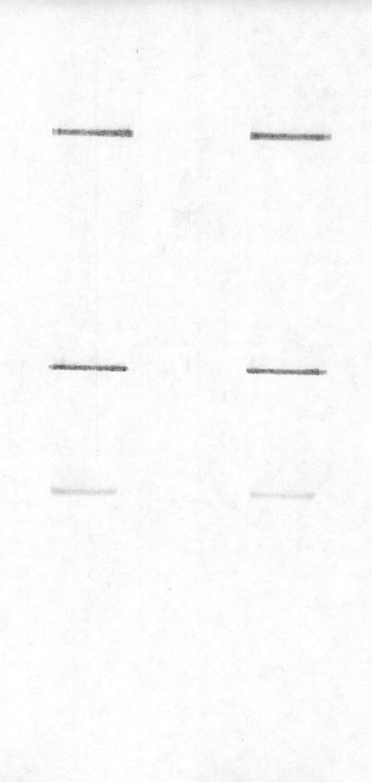

ALSO BY SAM SAX

Bury It

Madness

All the Rage

STRAIGHT

sad boy / detective

A Guide to Undressing Your Monsters

PIG

POEMS

Sam Sax

SCRIBNER
New York London Toronto Sydney New Delhi

Scribner
An Imprint of Simon & Schuster, Inc.
1230 Avenue of the Americas
New York, NY 10020

This book is a work of fiction. Any references to historical events, real people, or real places
are used fictitiously. Other names, characters, places, and events are products of the author's imagination,
and any resemblance to actual events or places or persons, living or dead, is entirely coincidental.

First Scribner trade paperback edition September 2023

SCRIBNER and design are registered trademarks of The Gale Group, Inc.,
used under license by Simon & Schuster, Inc., the publisher of this work.

For information about special discounts for bulk purchases, please contact
Simon & Schuster Special Sales at 1-866-506-1949 or business@simonandschuster.com.

The Simon & Schuster Speakers Bureau can bring authors to your live event.
For more information or to book an event, contact the Simon & Schuster Speakers Bureau
at 1-866-248-3049 or visit our website at www.simonspeakers.com.

Interior design by Kyle Kabel

Manufactured in the United States of America

1   3   5   7   9   10   8   6   4   2

Library of Congress Cataloging-in-Publication Data has been applied for.

ISBN 978-1-6680-1999-3
ISBN 978-1-6680-2000-5 (ebook)

The creatures outside looked from pig to man, and from man to pig, and from pig to man again; but already it was impossible to say which was which.

—George Orwell, *Animal Farm*

table

STRAW

STICKS

PIG

STRAW

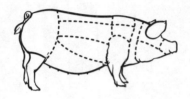

CUTS

head, loin, rump, shoulder, back fat, belly, neck,
ribs, picnic, jowl, shank end, clear plate, side,
spareribs, bacon, ham, hock, foot,
hind feet.

A BRIEF & PARTIAL HISTORY

the first pig wasn't a pig at all. was wild, *sus scrofa*.
practiced cannibalism, coprophagia. was named
darling in the garden & evolved from an ear of corn.
eve said pig & the world was. the first drawing
of any animal was made by a man using blood
& flowers to throw up the pig on a cave wall.
the first meal made from a pig was breakfast.
the last meal, supper. the first meal made for a pig
was all god's green earth, the acorn orchards
planted in jagged rows, the detritus of lesser species.
the word pig comes from the middle english picbred
meaning acorn, but pig existed before we had tongues
to name it. today we might call them soy & hormone
factories. the first book written about pigs was published
in 3468 BCE, the last will be this, until it isn't.
you who have but one mouth with which to take
apart meat, to name yourself & the inherited species,
do your work with care, as i have tried & failed here.
in the beginning pig offered its body so the world
might be built & when this world ends,
pig will inherit.

PIG BTTM LOOKING FOR NOW

i take pills & pass out in front of cameras.
an overdose on a live streaming jerk-off site

would be an embarrassing way to go
no matter who you are. they're angry i'm gone.

don't like to see a body emptied of its spirit.
draws attention to their own, body i mean.

would rather watch pleasure stampede through
a stranger like water through a hotel faucet.

we all leak behind screens. i close my eyes only to open
them on the same country. open them on a man

braying like a dial tone, a group of girls laughing
in tacoma, messages asking: you okay? you dying?

you dead? don't move. don't make a sound—
i close the computer. i go rinse my mouth.

LISP

there are more *s*'s in possession than i remembered / my name hinges
on the *s* / is serpentine / has sibilance / is simple / six-lettered /
a symbol / different from its sign / sound shapes how we think
about objects / the mouth shapes how sound spills out / how
the speaker's seen / a sigmatism is the homosexual mystique /
my parents sought treatments / i was sent to a speech / pathologist
/ sixth grade / a student / she gave exercises / i was schooled /
practiced silence / syllabics / syntax / my voice sap in the high
branches / my voice a spoonful of sugared semen / i licked silk
when i spoke / i spilt milk when i sang / when i sang sick men tore
wings from city birds / so i straightened my sound / into a masculine
i / the *s* is derived from the semitic letter shin / meaning my swishiness
is hebraic / is inherited / it's semantic / no matter what was sacrificed
/ the tongued isaac / a son against the stone of my soft palate / still
i slipped / my hand inside my neighbor's / waistband & pulled back
pincers / sisyphus with the sissiest lips / split-tongued suidae / sassy
& passing for the poisoned sea / now when i say please / may i suck
your cock / i sound straight / as the still second hand / on a dead
watch.

RAINBOW QUEEN ENCYCLOPEDIA

my ex wanted a pet pig, so we imagined it.
even gave the thing a name, rubbed its invisible head
before bed—

years later, on a rooftop, my ex confesses
she cheated on me: the city stretching out before us
filled with brightly locked doors.

the harm's far enough away i don't notice it.
a footnote swallowed ages ago. the pig would have been
beautiful—then grown too large for our small home.

would have needed more than us kids could offer
and then what needle would have ended us all
sobbing in the animal doctor's office;

blaming each other for the holes in the wall.
i'm glad we split when we did like a book
of hypothetical names. glad to have only suffered

in the imaginable ways. O Rainbow Queen
Encyclopedia, in some other world you are still
a pig-child dancing through immaterial fields

beheading tulips, snout rooting out heaven.
better to have only existed for a time in the imagination—
to never have to die.

BABE THE PIG DOES THE SHEEP-NOISE WHEN MOURNING ITS SHEEP MOTHER

grief is an animal. we all know that. but which animal
exactly? what kingdom, what family, is it ever a fish?

does its voice change as it leaves the body or is there
a bestiary somewhere in the chest?

great bone ark that crates and creates each heaving
lamentation. remakes the grieved thing as noise.

at the televised funeral the ingenue performs the gone
singer's living song and for a moment is overtaken

slow howl opening the painted cage of her mouth.
when S died i made sounds i haven't made since.

it came into me as wind. it rode me as wind

PORTRAIT OF DRAG QUEEN WITH A PIG NOSE
Oakland, 2019

\\

behind the gas station the queen begins facing away
from the crowd. low-cut back, floor-length gown. pulses
a knee to the music, arm on hip, believable human silhouette.
i should know this song. the rest of the audience sings along,
lit by a rented spot. bride to tires and oil. centuries pass
as she turns slow as a planet with all us dying on it. the reveal,
below the veil, her silicone snout, scarred and profound.
hybrid thing. elegant-bipedal-terrifying. think monster
but make it fashion. think what monsters go into making
fashion. we gasp at the temporary godhead standing
before us, the promise of all our science inside one passable
prosthetic. in a laboratory in california scientists inject human
stem cells into a pig fetus and for four weeks it lives.
miss vice, you are the perfected form of all our darkest
literatures smiling. you are the language we've been looking
for when we say we need a new language. darkness dragged,
bathed in light. the song ends. she sniffs. collects her tips.

SIC TRANSIT GLORIA MUNDI

my grandfather castrated pigs as a child
he tells me this casual as bread
when i bring up the book i'm writing

some thirty-odd years of talking
and this is the first that information raises its head
and shakes the mud from it

his father, i learn, was a farmer outside
baltimore. summers he'd be tasked with slicing
into piglets how one de-pits an avocado—

excising the sweet meats, seizing
their means of reproduction

how many pigs did you castrate, grandpa?
                            just a handful
and i picture hands the size of pastures
filled with castrato pigs singing opera oddly
        wagner probably

my grandfather wears shirts with buttons,
is freudian by training, obsessed with the germans
their brutalist art

i can hardly imagine him scolding a dog—

how is it we are always where we've been
even when unaware of it?

one moment you're drinking a cheap beer
in a velour jumpsuit and the next
you're descendant of jewish pig farmers

what would i learn if i were to write
this book on an entirely different subject:
antique clock repair, the sex lives
of astronomers, joy

A PIG PULLS US OUT OF PARADISE

the trip from l.a. was mostly N paraphrasing dante.
something about virgil being a punk-ass bitch.
that antique hell compressed enough to become comical.
we laughed even though we hadn't read it.
we smoked a thin and perfectly made blunt.
central valley somewhere north of bakersfield.
tomato fields in every direction, rows of red fruits.
since it's daylight the siren washes us first in noise.
then the speaker commands us to the shoulder.
paradise falling quick as ash. the officer wants.
to know if we knew how fast we were going.
where we're going so fast. N curses under her breath.
fucking pig, loud enough his mustache twitches.
what did you say, son? he asks me just like that, *son—*
the cement, bathed in daylight, refuses the cruiser's blues.
i smile so big he allows us to leave with a warning.
we force laughter again over all we haven't read.
abridged. inferno. purgatorio. paradiso. i can't stop.
trembling. can't not feel. each imperfection in the road.
magnified inside my expensive and tender teeth.

A VERY SMALL ANIMAL
@ *The Lafayette Inn*

last night i took pictures of myself
in a borrowed leopard-print robe

in my head i was beautiful, the imitation
cat skin open as a novel at the middle

proust or some other lonely queer
whose obsessions make clean taxidermy

of the temporary body. disgusting to look
upon oneself in any capacity but especially

here—face rearranged in the split approximation
of pleasure. glamorous for a moment

then gone. it's not the lens but the living
who fathom eternity. my face so full

of wonder it's sick. how many men have
passed through this room, these lips?

INTERPELLATION

give me a name & i'll answer

  whenever a mother calls it out across the park

wanting only her child & not some tired queen

    sitting alone on a bench with a bottle

in a brown paper bag. but still i stand

  when hailed & say *excuse me, ma'am, did you call?*

& if not, what shall i do now i'm here?

names i've taken inside me like mouths

  full of stale bread. sip of water names

on airplanes over water. biblical names like a bridle.

  slurs like a bride.

    names i've bled out into clean bathrooms.

names i've assumed & ones others assumed

  were mine. he calls me baby & i am

preverbal & unvaccinated. boy,

  & i was. daddy & i split in half

like a common fish. pig & i slit my own throat.

in the throes a name can be a chicken bone

  or burning piano in the throat

calling down something larger

  into the bed or car or bathroom or

say my name & they all join us here,

                all the sams before me & all the sams

to come. say bitch

        & my mouth floods with painted dogs.

every christ, christian, jonathan.

           every lover, in one body. who i mean

when i say *you*. you made of letters.

                you sobbing behind the wheel

of your sobbing car. you showing up

           unannounced at my door.

when i say *you up* at four in the morning.

        when i say of youth i was never young.

if ever i texted too late begging

                for something ugly, forgive me.

i meant only to address the eternal

           beloved, who i thought was, for a moment,

haunting your phone. i who have been

           addressed & became. have lain

with men who never bothered

           with names & still, when it comes

time for it they always find

        something to say.

EASY FAST QUEERS
Yom Kippur

—to deny oneself hunger is to deny oneself—

—hunger is high glut & fructose syrup—

—cult of luxury & fried drive-through windows—

—life might indeed have ridden here on the back of a screaming
meteorite—

—but still here we persist in this annual trip around our sun—

—who throws its goodness upon us so we might grow grains to
fashion into pancakes—

—O pancakes! could there be a more perfect representation of the
circle—

—how we are returned to ourselves to feast, drenched in the sweet
blood-sap of trees—

—once a year my people fast—

—ask ourselves not to eat in the grease theaters of slaughtered
meat farms—

—to not cut the blushing necks of fruit stems—

—for one day to let nothing pass between our lips that isn't begging forgiveness—

—atonement is a word with the letter *o* buried inside, which is quite factually one perfect pancake—

—i make my annual catalog of misdeeds & sins, deny water & my mother, turn my suffering inward—

—apologize to everything, living & dead—

—in my youth i bttmed for gods & carnival goldfish alike—

—i knelt before false prophets & gargled bacon grease—

—i ate when i wasn't hungry—

—i have a hole in me—

—the hole swallows everything—

—i will be forgiven—

—nothing—

QUARANTINE À DEUX

a new app tells us whether it's safe to breathe
i haven't been outside in weeks

afternoons, sunbathe on the living room floor
beneath the barred windows

it's grown sepia out there
a filter descended over the true face of the world

the little man in my phone's purple today—wears a gas mask
recommends not riding a bicycle

i wipe ashes from my packages
my mail carrier says it's the end of the fucking world

if anyone, he should know: neither snow nor rain nor heat
nor gloom of night

almost two and half millennia ago we split brussels,
broccoli, kale, collards, kohlrabi, all from the same wild cabbage

such imaginations humans have
it's a miracle life existed here at all

long as it has

FOR MY NIBLINGS IN ANTICIPATION
OF THEIR BIRTH
for Sol & Ruby

my brother, knowing my work well, asked i not
include any references to semen in the throat
in this poem i'm writing you—so i shan't. instead:
semen in the books. semen in the leaves. semen
in the ground that grows the semen trees also
known as the callery pear. semen in the boat
that carried our family here. semen in the waters
where we left our dead. semen in the meadows
where we buried & bled. semen in the light
streaming through the stained glass of our synagogue
the image depicting an ark in an ocean of semen.
gossamer semen. octopus semen. garden of semen.
there are so many words for you children &
none of them are dirty—tho not all of them
are yours. now as you eat what your mother eats
her fear is your world torn & thrown to birds.
but still the light is thick in the trees. the callery
pears are loud this season & my throat is bright
with flowers for you both. such beautiful flowers
i hardly have the words.

ON THE TRUE RUMINANTS

the pig isn't & yet its hoof

is cloven how god wants it—

tho be wary the split foot

which draws a butcher in

not knowing the beast to be

monogastric as we speaking are—

why would any god want

our meat many-stomached?

seems arbitrary & yet

to ruminate means to consider

to chew this life into something

more digestible. a cow might

spend half its living just ruminating.

it's true, you are what what

you eat eats & how. how

many methods are there

of keeping the body clean?

that we experience joy

beside unspeakable suffering

must pass through the rumen,

reticulum, omasum, &

abomasum before being

absorbed by the bloodstream.

let us praise the pig instead

for saving its own damned self

from the executioner simply

by swallowing everything at once

once & for all. out in the fields

the true ruminants are lowing

attempting to make sense

of the grasses while the shohet

sharpens his blade & turns

his attention at last toward

the reader.

STICKS

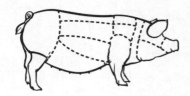

PRODUCTS

Phonograph Records: Violin Strings: Bone China
Drumheads: Leather Goods: Footballs: Cutting Oils
Antifreeze: Glycerin for Explosives: Linoleum
Pet Food: Marshmallows: Film: Industrial Lubricants
Matches: Sutures: Insulin: Drug Capsules
Heart Transplants: Chewing Gum

AUTHOR'S NOTE

i've never bred pigs. never fed pigs insects or anything vegetable. never bled pigs
with a sticking knife. never led pigs to the abattoir or slaughterhouse or to any house
of any kind. only read pigs. only begged to be pig-bred. only been called pig
a hundred times. only dead pigs on my plate or hanging in shop windows.
only cursed pigs from the back seats of suvs or wore a pig suit to the back rooms
of stank butcheries. was never awakened by their grunting deep into the night.
never rode atop a pig to the store for discount cigarettes. never castrated a hog
with bared teeth. never nursed one sick back to life at my own teat nor held
a pig infant squirming and pink in my outstretched palm. but once did look
into the eye of a pig behind a hardware store in brooklyn and saw reflected back
the blurred terror of this american world: children trembling between desks,
rows of mothers planting electronics, buildings rising along temporary coastlines
like chemical hair—

                    now

                                        i see
                i've stopped

                                        the animal
                eating

                                        everywhere
                the animal

CAPITAL

the market loves you

the market with its invisible hand   loves you

the market lifts the hem of your garment and speculates

the market bleeds   behaves erratic as a beehive doused in gasoline

the market ventures on diamonds and coffee beans

the market is volatile as the climate which is volatile because of the market

five little piggies went and were butchered one by one

the market exists for the fancy of financiers

market prices are fixed and nonnegotiable   sign here

the individual was invented to sell automobiles

a corporation is a synonym for an individual who dreams in rare earth metals

christ threw merchants out of his churches

today he can be worn around the neck for change

your suffering reverberates at the same frequency

as everyone else in your consumer-identity category

people are resilient as market trends

people are points on a grid

people throw themselves from buildings and bridges because of the market

the market loves you as data on a map

as something that eats

the market drinks jet fuel   shorts futures

the church passed laws that said jews were allowed to be

moneylenders only

and here we are, all of us, a few of us, most of us dead

the market knows what you want in bed

the thread count of your linens

the market wants you but not your opinions

doesn't want you to inquire into what money *is*

this little piggy went to market and returned to its repossessed duplex

this little piggy went to market and came back with half its meat harvested

this little piggy went into a field and became the market

vendors are currently hedging stock in its tenderloin

algorithms are being written out in back fat

O market   O maker

not long ago   at a school in chicago a few men sat around

an ornate wood table and hatched a plot in bloody mattresses

to set up a cage and called it data

wrote out equations to funnel monies off into imaginary rooms

and here we are all these years later eating crow calling it chicken

fellating war, famine, carbon emissions

O individual   don't be terrified, the market loves you

O maker

there is no bottom line

EPITHALAMIUM

X & X request the pleasure of your company at the celebration
of their union

to please god the wedding will be pareve
even if the marriage is doomed. the couple will reproduce
so many small tragedies, not least of all
their butterless cake. of course the children will come

out bruised. the light bulb breaks under the groom's foot
because even joy must be tempered. i look most jewish when crying
at weddings for the wrong reasons.
when organizing my books by date. when apologizing to trees

for the nature of paper. why these old laws
when my appetites now would be scorched from the earth
by even the gentlest old testament god?
if you train your body in restraint, pleasure finds its way

one way or another. X used to laugh as my tongue
traced maps across his stomach, then called me a faggot
behind my back. for so long i would not touch myself
for fear of finding a body.

i'm sorry i won't be able to make it to your wedding.

ANTI-ZIONIST ABECEDARIAN

after you finish
building your missiles & after your borders
collapse under the weight of their own split
databases
every worm in this
fertile & cursed
ground will be its own country. for us
home never was a place in dirt or even
inside the skin but
just exists in language. let me explain. my people
kiss books as a form of prayer. if dropped we
lift them to our lips &
mouth an honest & uncomplicated apology—
nowhere on earth belongs to us.
once a man welcomed me home as i entered the old city, so i
pulled out a book of poems to show him my papers—my
queer city of paper—my people's ink
running through my blood.
settlers believe land can be possessed
they carve their names into firearms &
use this to impersonate the dead—we are
visitors here on earth.
who but men blame the angels for the wild
exceptionalism of men?
yesterday a bird flew through an airport & i watched that border
zone collapse beneath its wings.

PIG BTTM LOOKING FOR THEN

the street is wealthy & well lit.
his apartment belongs to him—

the lawn's sprawling architecture
has its history. the trees, their history.

he was a man in my phone,
then a man above me, then a man

asleep. he looks different now
he's gone. unpressed. expressionless.

i bet he's dreaming uncomplicated
dreams. what buys this ease

to sleep with a stranger in your bed
or do i now somehow seem known

to him? having opened like the back
of a picture frame. having came

& stayed. what drove me here?
to seizure & breed? to become

again dis-ease's bride beside
an unconscious man.

a dozen similar apartments
the same memory foam mattress

this is the most tender i've felt:
how easily i could kill him

it is enough to let him sleep.

H1N1

the year the great swine craze swept the nation i was in pittsburgh
in a stranger's basement learning to middle-part my hair.

a flu gets its name how it moves. how it's redesigned incubating inside
this animal or that. this one, bred in factories, came out mean.

knowledge can be categorized this way, how it gets in you—a sneeze
or religion.   the first flu was influence,

was a serpent.   this flu moved like a whisper between cages, like newsprint
that sleeves and stains the throat. i was in pittsburgh, where nobody

knew my name—in a stranger's house who'd let me spend the night
in exchange for something sick. gagging in his fluorescent unfinished

basement, exchanging fluids as this new illness swept across the midwest
and found its way into me.   i showered and lungs came out.

wept lungs. spoke lungs. laid my head down upon his lung mattress
dreamt lung children throwing their own hands and feet.

i died that night in pittsburgh and arised one week later inside another
soft body speaking a language so old, no living thing is fluent.

the man gone. the media died down as it was assimilated
into the common vaccine and i left pittsburgh waiting

for the next great illness to wing or swim or sing its way toward us.

ERASURE OF THE GERASENE DEMONIAC

who hasn't lived

> howling & bruised
>> themself with stones?
>>> been chains in pieces
>> been many speaking
>>> unclean

cast in a   herd

drowned in the sea?

EVERYONE'S AN EXPERT AT SOMETHING

the more i learn, the more i learn
i don't know what the fuck
i'm talking about. someone
who doesn't care a fig for poetry
might think i knew a lot
yet in most bookshops i'm lost,
shelves heavy with the bodies
of forgotten writers. it's relative.
a president can say *audacity* or
a president can say *sad* & both eat
the slow-cured meat of empire.
when i say i carry my people
inside me i don't mean a country.
the star that hangs from my neck
is simply a way of saying israel
is not a physical place but can be
written down & carried anywhere.
it says my people are most beautiful
when moving, when movement,
when our only state is the liquid
state of water, is adapting to our container.
homeland sometimes just means
what books you've read, what stories
you spread with your sneakers.
my people, any place you live
long enough to build bombs
is a place you've lived too long—
it's relative. my friends, the only

thing i know for sure is the missiles
on television are only beautiful
if you've never known suffering.
my friends, the only country i will
ever pledge my allegiance to
is your music, is under investigation
for treason.

CHAZZER
for Sol

always enough	to eat	i ate
until i was	sick	left nothing
nothing left	for	next supper
my brother	who after	i snatched
the best rib	ate	what remained
	& grew	frail
there's	a hole	in me
always	has been	can't blame
ancestry	my family	any man
a hole	exists	only
to swallow	to grow	holy

TRUFFLE HOG

used to say i didn't believe in biology
which means clearly i was in university
too long—read too many books
by too many french deconstructionists,
too long in the humanities
attempting to live entirely in the brain
as if it weren't also meat—meat library—
meat commuter train. believed i was
only of language, set set of inheritances.
computer harvesting glands in service
of pleasure & pleasure's grieving twin—
treated the body like shit. smoked soda
bride. foil to flame. drank & cut to see
how the archive would open & shake.
some animals adapt to their circumstance.
others are adapted—you must know
what i mean. there is no nature outside
culture—i once read & nodded my head
like a dog being trained. humans learned
the truffle smells same to a pig as a boar
in heat & exploited her feasting. the fruited
fungi body buried three feet underground.
the sow's frantic digging, faux genital
pulsing oily in the earth. in retrospect
i should never have let him or him or he
do X or Z to me, shouldn't have begged,

pretended it was an experiment, grown
pleased by his feeding. a man & his animal.
the animal in its humanity. managing
to pull something wet & squirming
root-first from the dirt.

I HAVE AFFIXED TO ME THE DIRT
OF COUNTLESS AGES.
                    WHO AM I TO DISTURB HISTORY?
                                        Pigpen

how long without bathing at all? two weeks? six?
washing on special occasion

          in the kind houses of men. genitals & pits.
          the face unfaced with dish soap

or the putrescent pink stuff that affixes
to us the rock of ages.

               the liberal application of library hand sanitizer.
               cultivating my stink in theory. cultivating

my theory in stink. my bacteria farms.
politicized fragrances. faggot shit—

          alchemical, animal mix of where we've been
          & how we might carry each other

into our futures under stars that smell like god
knows what. me wanting nothing but a friend

               who would never try to fuck me while i slept.
               refusing aluminum—i who

ought have been robbed & robed in so
many armpits of america. before i'd ever been

      lost in the night, followed by someone
      who could not be reasoned with. the once

hitchhiking upstate where the man had
to cover his nose & so would not even try

           to touch me, blessed protective eau de toilette.
           how long refusing hot water?

how many times my glands plummeting
sulfurward? how long my mother left

      deodorants at my doorstep begging
      what have you done to my son,

      why do you insist on making yourself disgusting?

how to answer her without naming even the good
bacteria? scent yoked to memory, memory

      to skin, this whole holocaust of a country sweating
      antiseptics, landscape so strip-malled & blank

with bleach you have no choice but to leave
your stink on it.

AFTER THE PASSOVER SYNAGOGUE SHOOTING THE CONGREGANTS SING "GOD BLESS AMERICA" OFF-KEY

it's passover even on this airplane, where no angel
could pass unseen

on my little screen the killer charges *cultural marxism*—

marx, i read, who grew up in a split
jewish/goyish home, would sneak away over passover
to eat roast pork with his other half, my kind of jew.

who isn't split?

god bless america   they sing
discordant & corrosive through the white
buds breaking up the complimentary wi-fi   my sweet
     sweet   my hole   my gaping   my almost

on this the anniversary of my people's flight
from bondage
     on this the anniversary of marx eating pork

on this flight home i salt

water from the dry flat stones in my face
             watching the news
of one woman dead & the child next to me
     doesn't hear the police that will now forever be

stationed outside the synagogue
                    but only a sad man
traveling alone
            america passing below us

        i text S.   *most violence*
        is just people
                trying horribly
        to provide for their children

        & she asks

            really?   *do you really think that?*

EXPERIMENTS
September 2001

it could have been any american classroom
we sat behind bags of fetal pigs.

they wanted us to understand how the living worked
so we were going to take it apart. scalpel in hand.

they looked like children. a defeated man read
instructions from an old book. before exploring

beneath their skin the loudspeaker commanded
the televisions on & there the towers smoked

like fathers. what else could we do but leave
to call home? leave that room

preserved in formaldehyde for when we'd return
to this memory, finding the animal somehow alive

inside plastic, cut from our mothers
for the purpose of an american experiment

for the purpose of an american experiment
cut from our mothers

to this memory finding the animal alive
preserved in formaldehyde. we left home

like fathers. what else could we do?
the televisions where the towers smoke

beneath their skin. the loudspeaker commanding
instructions from an old book. before exploring

we looked like children. a defeated man reads
so we take him apart. scalpel in hand

they wanted us to understand how the living worked.
we sat behind bags of fetal pigs

it could have been any american classroom

IT'S A LITTLE ANXIOUS TO BE
A VERY SMALL ANIMAL

in an effort to save a dying language

we stockpile books   balanced on the edge of legibility
in the basement of a modern building
                    paid for by the dying

apply for grants to teach this old alphabet to children

an article on extinct insects lacks the accompanying audio
                         their songs are lost
outside how it's rendered in text
                    the phrases either make love or
set down a border   the letters sing there in the screen

light streaming out from inside the letters

something like 60 percent of species gone since we started counting

in the city, the library takes   poems from children
        in dying towns around the globe
& sets them to music

this project is funded by the same government
that bankrupted their soil & currency

in order to correspond with the divine, darwin drew the shapes
of plants & animals in a book

mendel, the father of genetics, had no children

yiddish is a language until it isn't

we wouldn't understand middle english today if we heard
it at the bar   tho might if screamed by soldiers

inside the natural history museum beside the insects & tortoises
are dioramas of people

the mannequins frozen in living portraiture: praying to gods,
walking on legs, digging in dirt

                    the names of jews are stenciled
onto the gallery walls & it is this money that has kept us
on this side of that border

in an effort to save a dying species, scientists are trying to dim
the sun   scientists are making use of graphs & new medias
scientists are burying seeds in vaults
                                    within the earth

in the basement of a modern building, in a pressure-controlled room
the books are being studied by children   the books
        will be there   until they aren't
until there are not eyes left to read them

right now the children are translating the story of a girl
who in hiding from a god   is transformed into a tree

& we think: yes, yes exactly.

NEARLY EVERY INVADING ARMY BROUGHT PIGS WITH THEM TO FEED THEIR SOLDIERS

they reproduce so quick generations could be eaten during a single siege.

adaptable they followed, devouring towns and forests, so soldiers ate

the worlds they invaded. even after illness swept through the men like wind

through a grain silo, the pigs they left behind, killing the hillside, remain.

HEADLINES

"literature is news that stays" —*Some Pig*

in an iowa pork plant managers bet
on how many workers will get
the new illness. in taipei thousands
take to the streets to protest US
pork imports. in missouri residents
worry the new pig farm will damage
public lands. in 2030 plant-based
pork sales are predicted to surge.
in iowa new research examines
the speed of pneumonia. in cape
cod authorities declare "dead pig
not killed in skater gang ritual."
in order to prepare the head for
consumption you must first boil it
down to a thick jelly. in some cases
the pandemic spurs automation
at the abattoirs. infertile pigs are put
down according to an algorithm.
in the year i was born the pork
industry coined the slogan "the
other white meat." in the year
my family immigrated—in illinois
a barn fire kills ten thousand. in the film
the prom queen responds not well
to the pig blood dropped on her
from heaven. in a tweet a man
asks, *how do I kill the 30-50 feral hogs*

that run into my yard within 3-5 mins while my small kids play? in the *financial times* bull market run in lean hog futures still strong. in west texas feral sounder upends township. in the 1800s thousands of pigs roamed wild the streets of Manhattan. in 2018 i do the same, wild turkey in my jacket, deciding whether to dive into traffic. in 1969 the yippies run pigasus. in santa rosa pig blood's smeared on the defense witness's door. in my body i do my best to record plainly the facts of the day. in an iowa pork plant seven are fired for betting on how many workers will get sick. in an iowa pork plant over one thousand people contract the illness, leaving at least six dead.   in a small city east of here, wild pigs have overtaken the pigs at the police station. in some better future more wilderness will come do the same.

SAVAGING PIGLETS

✂- -

write the name of the person you love most

_____

cut out this page

& eat it

BRICKS

EXCERPTS FROM FICTIONAL PIGS

god of war. odysseus's man who chose to stay. monk's pet. depression pig.
pig from cincinnati who's able to dance. who's a hybrid of a man, a bear, a pig.
a phantom with red eyes. who tries to get famous. villainous wild boar.
well-mannered and the runt. who led the animal revolution and established
a dictatorship. a bank. a boar god, corrupted by an iron ball lodged in his body.
also known as "king mudbeard." who dies at the start of the story. the best
friend. tiny timid character. hyperintelligent species, genetically modified
to grow human organs. accomplice of napoleon. nameless pigs who serve
as a satirical metaphor. mutant warthog. a trio of siblings. a stuttering pig.
a pig who finds out why he is being bred and decides to eat the farmer.

HOG LAGOON

you can smell it soon as you enter the state

caught from space the pools look like wounds in the earth

cut precise and surgically pink

hundreds of millions live and die inside the factory

waste falls through the slats and slices into pits

stored in the open to be sprayed onto crops

which are fed to the pigs' children

                              pink viscous circle

some humans mistake the spray for rain

some children open their mouths to catch faith on their tongues

the rain makes its way into homes even with the windows closed

makes its way into rivers and lakes

what happens inside the factory can never stay inside the factory

no matter what the farm believes it pays

no matter how thick the walls

                                    we all eat shit

everything that happens on earth happens everywhere

comes up in us as fungus

we won't taste until we're dead

SQUEAL LIKE A PIG

this is how men were
meant to touch
i believed
humiliating daylight
on film
learned by watching
i could be
either a city boy
lost in wilderness
or a wilderness
lost in a city
boy tied to witness
boy hurting
boy hurt
never imagined
i could leave
become the trees
eating light
while all these men
blur & dilate
around me

ETYMOLOGY

in the beginning there was a beginning & before that it'd already begun
& before that

a gun

every story i love begins with violence. every story ends.

a life undone as a button slid through the winged gap in its fabric.
little portal opening into light into a bald chest bared as a fang

the etymology of gun is wonderment   from the dutch

from my uncle's locked cabinet he shot out over the city of los angeles
laughing to impress as i sassed lavish in my black jeans

the etymology of gun is hunger   from the french

from the waistband of a strange man's madness as he traced
my outline down an unlit louisville street

from the greek

fired from a passing car through my neighbor's window entering
his brain & refusing to leave—

from the old english

a man enters an orlando nightclub   breathes

the etymology of gun is police is greed is country   from the german

from the sea

almost gossip outside my barred window
almost the falling sound of metal leaves

from the old country

my mother's town where the gun store on the corner's the only business
not out of business

from the new country

where a weapon can be shipped to your doorstep next day

the etymology of gun is tied to horses   from the old norse

a woman's proper name   made of two words for battle

i held a gun only once, my lover begged me to press it
against the back of his head as we fucked, his pistol fit so easy

in my hand when i pulled the trigger, the sound it made
swallowed me

click.   .   .   .   .

LEX TALIONIS

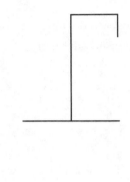

it's true what you've heard
pigs once stood trial for breaking
the laws of men. a sow, accused of eating
the face off a sleeping infant,
might have been arraigned in court
with full ceremony. a lawyer assigned.
& when found guilty of the crime,
maimed, dressed in human clothes,
then hanged by its feet to die,
which was, as you've likely heard too,
the same punishment
reserved at the time for jews

POEM WHERE THE WRITER SEES THEMSELF IN AN OLD PHOTOGRAPH

they cut off our hair & there we were, hairless. a photograph
in a history i skimmed so quick, i missed. we were there less
than elsewhere. cut so close the scalp gleamed. a row of six
pixelated moons. blood rose to its feet. our hair, not ours,
once separated like a fingernail. gold from our teeth. there
on the page. a camp. a cage. right angles. impossible. sharp
as a fade. razors in drag. black boots & blades. i pull the image
up on my screen. thumb the six bare heads. sex organs.
my face. my face. i'm alive of course because others died &
i'll be survived by no one [amen] [amen] my gift to this planet,
extinction. the singed end of a family line. today a man sits
beside me at the piano & plays a song with my name, the one
where a man's rendered powerless by the woman who takes
his hair. even here with his breath a flat iron, i'm standing
between twin pillars, my arms' cargo, hardly mine. when
he's done i take him to bed. take his family into my darkroom
apologizing [i'm sorry] again & again [i'm sorry] [i'm sorry]
though i can't quite say why.

POEM WRITTEN INSIDE A LEATHER PIG MASK

only a blade of light makes it
through the eye-slit to the eye.
inside sweat from the living
dances with the dead's tanned
stank. in the leather shop south
of market i run my hands over
the animal heads in back behind
the harnesses & straps while
two men now surely dead
perform at pleasure on a screen:
the scene is military, the men are sweet.
alone, i palm the pig head & hold it
aloft only to slide it over me,
a grandmother's dress & am
transposed & transpossessed back
inside the living cow in its lake
of cows outside some missouri
township all knowing they would die
but none imagining they might be
remade into the perverted image
of a different living animal
then worn by a man wanting
to be regarded as livestock.
right now this is the queerest thing
i can imagine: the animal yearning
within the animal within the animal.
child who dreams of growing
into a swan only to wake in terror

at a mouth filled with feathers.
i've never been lonelier than i am
right now, inside this pig mask
made out of a cow, watching
these men break into each other
again & again, two men
who will never die.

THREE STORIES

in the end, the children come to learn, the beast lives in them.

in the end, it is the animal's proximity to language that saves him.

in the end, despite their best intentions, the pigs become men.

PEDAGOGY

now she's gone my teacher wants to know
where the speaker enters the poem

the wind blows open the screen door & it catches
on its chain. out back my neighbors are smoking

a pig to make it last. my teacher only became
my teacher after she passed. before that

she was a woman who had lived a long time.
as always i am an ungrateful child, a student

first of ingratitude. ungracious as a wasp. a knot
in a history of rope your hands don't notice

as you hold on for dear life. dear life, the speaker
is the chain holding the door closed & the wind

is my teacher, the smoke curing meat.
my teacher had stories about all the dead poets

which made her, while living, prophetic. proximity
is next to godliness. for a woman who had no use

for music or pleasure her writing beats the page
until knuckles singe. my speaker wants to know

when the teacher enters the poem, if she ever leaves,
if she's always there in the text, shaking her heads,

cutting the weeds.

PORCHETTA DI TESTA
or ROLLED-UP PIG FACE

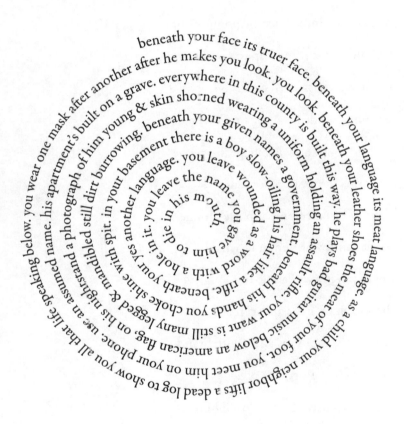

beneath your face its truer face. beneath your language its meat language. as a child your leather shoes the mear of your music. below an american flag. on his night. use an assumed name. his apartment's built on a grave. everywhere in this county is built this way. he plays bad guitar. a photograph of him young & skin shorned wearing a uniform holding an assault rifle. your want is still many legged & mandibled still dirt burrowing. beneath your given names a government. beneath your basement there is a boy slow-oiling his hair like a rifle. beneath his hands you choke shine with spit. in your yes another language. you leave wounded as a word with a hole in it. you leave the name you gave him to die in his mouth. you wear one mask after another after he makes you look. you look. you look. like speaking below. your neighbor lifts a dead log to show you all that life. you meet him on your phone.

JAMES DEAN WITH PIG
Dennis Stock, Life *Magazine*

even without the image you can see it.

dean, black-booted, bedroom-eyed,

hair coiffed into its iconic pompadour.

he holds a hat turned up to the sky.

sty littered with corn husks. big animal

standing beside him. i've never seen

his films but know his shape. his name

performs the work of looking.

this photo taken on a trip back home

to the family farm in indy. what life

might have been had he not sought

the spotlight. [the apocrypha

i love best, about his affair with brando.

sub & dominus. god & pig.

they met on set. dean so loved him

he held him up like a father

& brando did what he wanted, put out

cigarettes on the boy, used a belt.]

this photo's taken in 1955 & it's unclear

whether he carries the terror & pleasure

to come or if it's waiting somewhere

beyond the lens. if he returned

to the farm knowing or if he returned

to the farm known. now both are dead—

one leaves behind films, the other only

meat & children, who perhaps

you, dear reader, have eaten

& in that eating

took pleasure.

at the bottom of the well
a   boy   is   singing
the   boy   sings   well
from   the   bottom
from the deep bottom
of his weather from
the weathered bottom
of   his   depths
the well is a song
the   boy   inherits
by falling the boy
who fell felled himself
leapt down the well's
throat   the   well
is the world turned
inward the boy leapt
when   he   heard
himself echoed back—
his whole life beside
windows   beside
telescopes the boy
never could imagine
becoming the heard
thing till he heard it
the   whole   town
worried   for   him
when he fell but not
when he became it—

endless   dark   jacket,
long-dead   alphabet
he swallows & swallows
the whole world is a well
& all men are buckets
dropped   into   him
the boy grows large
through   swallowing
poisons the ground-
water belts through
the town's wet taps
at dawn he laughs
looking up at the red
coin   the welt
he left   on a god's
heaving chest.

THE COCK

you can't spell basement without semen.
or i suppose you could but then it'd just read *bat*.

somewhere south on second avenue's a staircase
you pay ten dollars to descend onto a dance floor

tho more a dark field of men who've already removed
their heads so as to blend into the eternal body

which is always loosening & welcoming fluids. what becomes
of the indivisible soul in basements such as this?

here where the spirit is passed around as a yawn or religion.
soul i say, welcoming someone me yet not

into this rented & temporary skin when an oddly cold erection
nuzzles its wet nose into my palm like an elderly dog.

in that old story the three-headed dog guards the gate
to the world of the dead. in this underworld, it's the living

STREET FAIR

at folsom i watch one man bind another

in blue saran

the sub positioned in the shape of a shamed christ

his hole exposed to the sun as crows circle

his back bruised gray as a grandfather's cadillac

the dom orbits in a black latex mask

this ritual as old as the day is

as these two upon the dais rosed in prayer

i participate in the spectacle by looking

it's clear they like to be seen

grappling in this performance of power & suffering

it's clear we like to be looking—congregants & gentiles alike

i too have been bound & done the binding

too have stood upon stages & taken my licks

none of this is new

but it's easier to make the holy novel

to holy anything for the occasioning of a poem

haven't yet figured how to accept it's grown a bit boring

or that i have—that age may well have unwed me to depravity

a queer public flogging offering up nothing but a yawn

but a fist unfurling into nice-smelling soaps

that i walk through back rooms now like the ghost of a ghost

so here in this crowd of heretics i will to be fleshed back

to be disgusted into beauty

anything fishnet—leather—taped crosses over the eyes—

clamps & plugs & electrocutions—nitrates & sounding metal—

& at last turn my head to see the boy in his pig mask

kneeling in the bright gutter beside the row of urinals

begging to be made clean

as a man in a gold harness unzips

produces himself & empties onto his pig face

light reigning down—

& i well up along with the boy

as i am become a well with a boy at its bottom

& when he is done we rise together from the water

as he presses his wet carapace against the dry

& both are in this one moment undying

my gaze wanders back to an old woman in her folding chair

dressed in black distressed denim

smiling with a riding crop

she uses to conduct the crowd in & out of pleasure

& i've found me,

a part of & apart from at once

in a filthy lawn chair overlooking my own life

then her eyes are upon me

XENOTRANSPLANTATION

my friend's got a pig heart in him.
my friend's got part of a pig's heart,
a piece, his heart's part pig.
the aortic valve is the dog-god
guarding the tube blood runs
through once it's been scrubbed
clean. one of two semilunar
valves, which sounds like a part
of a moon, a piece. my friend's
got moons in him separating
the two major atria. my friend's
full of ballrooms, those dark
vaulted ceilings. my friend's a vegan.
my friend's a vegan with a pig heart
thumping club music. my friend
believes the pig in him is vegan
since it eats what he eats,
speaks when he speaks. the pig
heart pulses in his chest
like a reflection of the moon
in a puddle out behind the club
once we've finished dancing.
my friend takes drugs so his body
doesn't reject the organ. my friend
takes drugs so he can go on
dancing. his pig grown to be
sewn into a man's ribs, unnaturally
selected, no god could have

predicted this in any garden.
still holy the bit of tissue
that lets him live & live.
thin filament that set another
seventeen years going inside him.
if you listen with one ear
to his chest you can hear
the pig heart singing, calling
out to any listening animal:
all i. want is. to live. & live.
& live. & live. & live. & live.

MISS PIGGY

great porcine drag queen

you who grew erudite in the slaughterhouse shadow

eyelashes like black swords teased up to challenge heaven

eternal in your powdered foundation

refusing every day the knife's inevitable & unkosher ending

be-snouted fount of youth! seminal queer iconoclast!

pearls to bed, pearls in the junkyard, pearls on television

diva of late night, of talk shows, of prime time

door-kicker for the nonconventional romance

shown us how to love across identities arbitrary as phylum & species

bless that impossible coupling!

how you took an entire frog inside you & remained the same bad pig!

who'd karate chop anyone dumb enough to disrespect   *HI-YA*

what little faggot wouldn't look upon you & be seen or saved or salved?

you who never questioned you were destined for stardom

O miss miss! O great swine demimonde! O dame pig!

i'm yours till i end   you, my religion   how i understand us all now

we are ourselves & the hand inside that guides us

we who are given voice by that same spirit that gives voice

to everyone you have ever loved

IT'S A LITTLE ANXIOUS TO BE A VERY SMALL ANIMAL ENTIRELY SURROUNDED

the world was already [young|sick|lost] when we came to it
we were busy looking [for|at|through] god
when we went to the dance we brought our new [shoes|father|flask]
borrowed a [shirt|religion|mask] & sat in the bleachers
[music|oil|trash] filled our rivers
stayed up for the after[party|life|math]
the forests were [protected|sold|ash]
we wrote [letters|checks|ads] against corruption
blamed [science|systems|depression] for our cities
when the [oceans|fires|droughts] came
when the [rain|bomb|flu] came
when the [weather|weather|weather] came
we [weathered|welcomed|watered] it
we were [prepared|shocked|responsible]
please for one line look nowhere else
who made our [life|language|living] here
whoever eats [rivers|ash|lambs] will return
each time we turn our mouths to [sob|scream|song]
children are blameless as they become [gone|ghosts|gods]

ODE TO THE BELT

it's clear the future does not bode well for the living

my man won't let me forget where leather comes from

the engineered animal bent over in chemical grass

the slit thing hanged & blood slunk   skin stripped

& tanned in order to keep a man decent   i know

how to keep a man the belt knows how to keep order

the sound of his unbuckling's pavlovian, a sidewalk

split into drooling meat. he beats me into my evening

blush, i clutch pearls, eyes the color of a little red cloak

bless this bridle wrapped around my throat while he

bloods me, bless the constricted windpipe's unlikely music,

bless any thing that can be remade to eke pleasure

from stone, O bless all this life thrashing against death's

garish precipice, O bless me lord, bless me doorman,

bless me cormorant & courtship & torture & husbandry,

give me enough compression to remember i once lived here

& i'll accept in the end not even death will wife me

IT'S A LITTLE ANXIOUS TO BE A VERY SMALL ANIMAL ENTIRELY SURROUNDED BY WATER
   —Piglet

what will be left after the last fidget
spinner's spun its last spin

after the billboards accrue their thick
layer of grit masking advertisements
for teeth paste & tanqueray gin

after the highways are overtaken
by invasive forests

after the rabbis leave their congregations
for drink

after new men rise to lead us sheep
toward our shearing, to make bed-
sheets from our hair

after the high towers have no airplanes
to warn away & instead blink purely

toward heaven like children
with one red eye

after phone lines do nothing
but cut the sky into sheet music
& our phones are just expensive
bricks of metal & glass

after our cloud of photographs collapses
& all memories retreat back
into their privatized skulls

after the water taps gasp out their final
blessing

what then?

when even the local militias run
out of ammunitions

when the blast radiuses have been
chalked & the missiles do all they were
built to

when us jews have given up our state
for that much older country of walking
& then that even older religion of dirt

when all have succumbed to illness
inside the church of our gutted pharmacies

when the seas eat their cities

when the ground splits like a dress

when the trash continent in the mid-atlantic
at last opens its mouth to spit

what will be left after we've left

i dare not consider it

instead dance with me a moment
late in this last extinction

that you are reading this

must be enough

Th-th-th-that's all, folks!

acknowledgments

Poems in this collection have been previously published in The Adroit
Journal, The American Poetry Review, The Atlantic, bath magg, The
Collagist, Dispatches magazine, Foglifter, Fourteen Poems, Granta,
Guernica, The Nation, Poem-a-Day, Poetry, Poetry London, The
Rumpus, Tin House, *and* The Yale Review.

Deep gratitude to everyone who's offered feedback on these poems
or talked to me about pigs over the past six years, and everyone who
sent me pig art, pig articles, or pig artifacts.

Thanks to Micheal for making so much of this life possible.
Thanks to Suzan for doing the same. Biggest gratitude to Hieu and
Paula and Cameron and Franny and Fatimah and Danez and Safia
and Charif and Kaveh and Nate and Alison for being my family.
Big gratitude to Kim & ITALIC. Love to my gone teachers and
the ones still here. Thanks to my cohort at the Stegner Fellowship
and everyone else who spent time with these poems. Thanks to my
family, blood and otherwise. Thanks to Kathy and Rob for making
this book happen and to everyone at Scribner. And lastly, to all the
farmers and scholars of the pig—it's been an honor to make these
poems in the shadow of your work.

"A Brief & Partial History": The earliest drawing of a creature ever was identified in 2021 as a 45,500-year-old drawing of a swine on the Indonesian island of Sulawesi.

"Lisp" borrows its form from speech pathology exercises.

"Sic Transit Gloria Mundi" ("Thus Passes the Glory of the World") is for Albert.

"Easy Fast Queers" is indebted to hunger and Anis Mojgani.

"Quarantine à Deux" was written during the intersection of the COVID-19 pandemic and the California wildfires.

"Author's Note" mentions Franklin the pig, who often resides behind Crest Hardware on Metropolitan Avenue in Brooklyn.

H1N1 is swine flu, which I caught in 2009 in Pittsburgh.

"Everyone's an Expert at Something" references a particularly heinous on-air comment from Brian Williams.

The final lines of "It's a Little Anxious to Be a Very Small Animal" reference a line by Cameron Awkward-Rich and an idea from CAConrad and D. A. Powell.

In "Headlines," *Some Pig* is an abbreviation of Ezra Pound, and most of the text is culled from news headlines from 2020–2022.

"Savaging Piglets" refers to a process by which mother pigs eat their children in captivity so the children won't have to experience unlivable conditions.

Court information for "Lex Talionis" comes from *Animal Trials* by Edward Payson Evans.

"Poem Written inside a Leather Pig Mask" was largely written in Mr. S Leather.

"Pedagogy" is for Eavan.

"The Cock" borrows a line from Martín Espada.

"It's a Little Anxious to Be a Very Small Animal Entirely Surrounded" borrows its form from Emily Dickinson's Letters.

about the author

Sam Sax is a queer, jewish writer and educator. They're the author of *Madness* (2017), winner of the National Poetry Series, and *Bury It* (2018), winner of the James Laughlin Award from the Academy of American Poets. They're the two-time Bay Area Unified Grand Slam Champion, with poems published in *The New York Times*, *The Atlantic*, *Poetry*, *Granta*, and elsewhere. Sam's received fellowships from the National Endowment for the Arts, the Poetry Foundation, and Yaddo, and is currently serving as a lecturer in the ITALIC program at Stanford University. Their first novel, *Yr Dead*, will be published by McSweeney's in 2024.

COLOPHON

this book is set

in a history of speaking.

a font is more

than baptizing water

than an oil reservoir

in a lamp. it asks

only: do you know

what i mean? & if not speak

it back to me so

i might understand

more clearly